Flow in Everyday Life

Sujit Hemadri

ISBN 978-93-5458-663-7

Published in India 2021 by Pencil

A brand of

One Point Six Technologies Pvt. Ltd.

123, Building J2, Shram Seva Premises,

Wadala Truck Terminal, Wadala (E)

Mumbai 400037, Maharashtra, INDIA

E connect@thepencilapp.com

W www.thepencilapp.com

Author biography

Sujit has a deep interest in understanding Human Behavior. This is the first book among many more books to come. It is this deep interest to understand the Human Behavior, that he has written this book which comes out of observations from everyday life

Sujit has gone through a troublesome route in his life which has made him learn life skills from experience. It is these experiences and observations which has made him write this book. Sujit strongly believes in exploration which helps us to learn lessons which are not apparent

Sujit believes that this book helps people in staying happy in the present moment and be in joy. Good health and happiness are the core ingredients for a joyful life

CONTENTS

Preface

Each one of us is unique in how our body is built and how our minds work. Each one of us builds a persona by the continuous interactions that we have with the outside World, which includes people, other living beings and non living objects. Our Mind has a very important role in this continuous interaction with our surroundings, which is sometimes observed in stressful behaviors like Fear, Anxiety, Assumption, Procrastination etc which drains our energy. We are sure you can relate to these behaviors

Our Mind without any precursor goes into thinking mode relating to the current actions happening around us. Be it a happy situation, a frightening situation or an emergency situation, our Mind starts thinking about the situations imaging ourselves in it. Haven't you observed this behavior?

If it is a happy situation, our Mind thinks about the situation with us as the person in the situation. It doesn't stop there! The Mind tries to imagine various situations in addition to the current situation as probable forthcoming situations. Quite an imaginary World, isn't it?

If it is a troubling situation, the Mind thinks about the situation with us as the person in the situation. Needless to say, the thinking extends into further probable troubling situations arising out of the currently thought about situation. It is a loop, can't you see it?

Here is an interesting fact! The Mind is so cleverly designed that it takes situations which are thought about, as real and manipulates into body behavior! If it is a happy situation, the Mind makes the body release hormones which elicit relaxation and happiness. If it is a troubling situation, the Mind makes the body release hormones which elicit fear and stress!

The Mind has the ability to turn thoughts into bodily behaviors, which can prove to be unhealthy for both the Mind and the Body. How does it do that?

Go on and read this Book! We have illustrated daily examples to explain the Mind's influence on the Body

Introduction

"Is our Mind a Monkey?" That's the question the book starts with. The analogy is that our Minds behave the same way as that of a Monkey who is never stationary in one place. We are sure you will be able to relate our Mind's behavior to a monkey's in the first chapter

From there on the book relates stories on the workings of the mind. We advise readers to imagine themselves in these stories and imagine how they would have reacted to situations mentioned therein. The book relates stories from three aspects of Life. Interactions within Home and Family, at the Workplace and in the Society, which we believe covers most of the interactions we have on a daily basis

Later on the book delves deep upon how the mind works in the areas of information and thoughts. We touch upon the aspect of Chaos, which we experience on a daily basis. We illustrate how Action can be a sword against thoughts. We give a Baby's example, a Monk's example and the Nature's example in relating how each one of these remain extremely aware in their Actions and day-to-day Living

We go on to relate Mind-Body coordination and how we can modulate the Mind's influence on Body expressions. We even go deep in trying to correlate Medicine to Awareness which we feel is a very interesting area. We also relate how Awareness can create Freedom of the Mind, which is the most important Freedom we all need

The chapters following later on helps us in how we can achieve a Flow to our Lives. The writings help us on how to be aware in the moment. We have also opened up on how Living has to be the most important Action for all of us. We have also touched upon the concepts of Compassion and Love to solve the unnecessary behavioral tensions which arise between Human Beings

The last few chapters help us relate to how to be aware in the moment. We have written about how Awareness is the most effective tool to be Productive in our day-to-day Life

We are sure that the book will help you to closely watch your own behavior in day-to-day Life and work towards avoiding the unnecessary stressful situations in our Lives

Relating our Mind to a Monkey

Is our mind a monkey? Don't know what to say? Well, it does look like that. What does a monkey do? It does not stick to one place, keeps jumping from one branch of the tree to the other and often troubling people around. Mind, mostly does the same

But, with the mind, it is about thoughts. Mostly irrelevant thoughts right from the time you wake up. "Did I sleep well?" ; "Let me sleep for some more time!" ; "I don't like to go for a jog!" ; "That movie was great yesterday" ; "I have a deadline at work today" ; on and on and on! I am sure you can relate

Have you wondered why thoughts appear in the mind? If you clearly observe, it is the protective instinct of the mind trying to keep you protected. If you observe, the moment you wake up, the mind tries to remember what was the last thing you did the previous night to make sure we are in continuity. The mind tries to keeps us in protective mode, by trying to make sure we are relevant in the current context and there is a continuity to our existence

The most powerful tool the mind has, is the ability to store information. Everything you see, hear and experience through your senses gets registered into your mind's storage house. The mind keeps relating to similar experiences in the past that are happening currently. Here comes your dejavu moment!

The mind, either tries to think about the past or the future. It keeps relating current experiences with either the past or the future. If something bad is currently happening, the mind straightaway goes and relates it to similar experiences in the past or it tries to conjure up future experiences. If you are traveling by train, your mind remembers earlier experiences by itself and tries to relate. It is then that you talk to people about it later. The initiation is automated!

The most funny part is your mind starts playing songs sometimes or enacting a scene from a movie you watched or remember a situation based on the similarity of our current experience. Quite mysterious and difficult to understand. Your mind tries to relate to the memories and the information stored in your brain. It appears that our mind, by doing such an act, tries to keep us involved in something. My mind tries to get into thoughts of improvement, while I write this!

This book tries to help you get around the problem of a thinking mind by being aware of it. We try to narrate day to day stories which you can relate to and learn from

Stories at Home and Family

1

The sun was shining bright. It was a typical extremely hot summer day. The lady's mother was roaming around in the garden after breakfast. She was quite old with regular medications

The lady suddenly heard a sound from the outside. Her mother had fallen unconscious. The lady was anxious and jittery. Her mind started working, relating the experience to the previous experiences she had seen. 'Is there a cardiac problem? What might have happened?' Her mind went about thinking all unwanted circumstances instead of attending to the present requirement

The neighbor rushed and sprinkled water on the old lady's face. She became conscious. By then, fifteen minutes had passed. The neighbor made the old lady drink some water and gave her some electrolyte water which made her feel good. The neighbor guessed it might be due to dehydration that the old lady fell unconscious and asked the daughter to take her mother for a regular check-up

What the neighbor guessed was right! There was nothing wrong with the health of the old lady. It was due to dehydration that the old lady went unconscious. Quite a relief! The daughter then realized about the unnecessary thoughts that came to her mind previously. She realized the importance of action through the experience

Fear is closely associated with thinking. It is the incessant thinking which induces fear. "What if?" applies to all situations. The mind incessantly projects future happenings. And they do look like possible outcomes. But, are they?

It is only when you act on it, that you get to know. Repetitive tasks are different. You tend to know the outcome given the input. But that doesn't restrict the mind from getting busy! It continues to think. What if you took a dip in ice cold water? Take the dip first!

So, Action does look like a possible answer to restrict the Mind from thoughts. But, is it enough? No! Bad Habits are difficult to forego! The Mind will tend to get back to its ways of getting into unwanted thinking mode. Then, how do we restrict it?

2

A woman had been married to the person whom she felt she loved. They both were soon going to have a baby in their family. All the needs looked to be fulfilled. Yet the woman felt a void which was not filled

The woman had not gotten out of her previous relationship. She was physically out of it, but she still felt the void emotionally. Due to this, she felt her marriage to be incomplete sometimes, despite that she had married a person whom she felt she loved. She was in the midst of a lot of developments in her current family, yet she was troubling herself with her past. The husband was a very practical man, who understood human behavior to a fair amount. Seeing his dull wife, the husband tried to peel out the layers of this behavior by asking sensible questions. The woman revealed that her past relationship was troubling her. The husband got the clue. Being a person understanding human behavior, he subtly made his wife understand that staying in the present is the most righteous act she can do in such a period. The husband promised that he will make the necessary changes to interact more with her so that she doesn't feel the void.

Slowly, the wife started to appreciate her current companion and progressed happily in welcoming the baby. The husband helped her to stay in the present

We remember experiences and emotions in the past which trouble our present. It is our minds which make us remember the past experiences when similar experiences happen in the present. The mind gets into thinking mode which only obstructs us from absorbing the present experiences completely. Such instances are related to a whole lot of other experiences, both positive and negative

Do you feel such thoughts are interfering with your present experience? What do you do?

3

Two married sisters were cooking for their family gathering. The house was very active with kids making noise around and elders talking about their life. Each of these sisters were trying to discuss and decide the menu for the midday lunch. They discussed on some dishes to be prepared and started discussing on how to prepare it

They started to tell each other how each of them prepared those dishes at their own home. Each one had their own reasons as to why the process of their own cooking was good. They reached a point where they started arguing as to why each one should accept the other's perspective. Voices started increasing in pitch. This was between the two of them. Then their father interrupted and asked what was the problem. Listening to the silly issue they were arguing on, he asked each one of them to divide the dishes between them. They prepared the food to eat and finished lunch. While on the table

each one of the sisters ate the dish prepared by the other sister. To each other's surprise, each one liked the dish prepared by the other sister more than how they would have prepared it themselves

After lunch, each one of the sisters appreciated the food prepared by each other and learnt how to prepare it from each other. Camaraderie spread between each of them and they realized how silly it was for them to argue on such small issues

Here also, it is the mind playing its role. Only if we are aware of the present moment and see the thoughts going on in our minds, can we control such silly situations. Ego is just an extended play of the mind. Do you agree?

Keeping our minds open for exploration is difficult. The information, memories and experiences stored in our brain most often acts as an impediment to exploration

4

It was 7am in the Morning with a rather dull outset with the Sun hiding behind the clouds that day. A man in his early 30's was a rather disciplined person with a daily routine to be followed. Somehow he had missed waking up at 5 am, the usual time he wakes up everyday. He was jittery getting up, not talking properly to his wife and parents.

He headed out to get some air and calm his mind, but his mind was already talking to itself. Thoughts of anger and frustration were talking to the mind. ``why couldn't he wake up today?. He was not able to calm his mind down. He went into a park which was greener than the normal parks he had seen around. He could hear birds chirping, with people walking and jogging around the park. He slowly closed his eyes and tried to concentrate on each of the sounds he was sensing. His mind slowly started to observe all the things happening around him. He could spot footsteps of people around him, observe the birds chirping, the sound of a distant train and the wind breezing past his face. His mind was able to observe and predict the distance of these objects as well! Quite an extraordinary resource, the mind is! Only if it is put to the right use!

The man sat still in the liveliness of the surrounding environment for half an hour. All his anxiety and thinking was gone. He was there at that moment feeling quite lively and fresh. He felt as though he went through a good night's sleep in those 30 minutes. He came back home greeted his wife and parents with a smile, served them tea and then got ready to the office and left with a smile on his face

Quite often, we tend to be bogged down by petty issues which do not affect us directly. But the mind makes trouble by getting into thoughts which are unnecessary. We tend to lose precious energy because of these thoughts and trouble the people we get along with on a daily basis. But, the solution lies in yourself. Only when we are aware of the present moment that we can absorb and respond to that moment in fullness

How aware are you now?

5

A young man in his late 30's was a staunch believer in astrology. His parents had benefited a lot by following astrological guidelines leading their life. They had taught the man how to follow the astrology guidelines in his daily life

The family was in preparation to get him married. They had started searching brides based on the birth charts. The man got to meet very few brides for first discussion, because of the in-depth search that the family was conducting. After all, all required conditions had to be met. The search went on for months, but the man hardly got to see a few brides. The man was frustrated. The man started to wonder whether such rituals are made to simplify life or to complicate them

The man had gone to meet one of his uncles at an old age home. He saw a girl there who was taking care of the people in the old age home. Caring for old aged people is a service done to God, they say. The girl did the work with such patience and a smile on her face that the man liked the way she handled situations around with such simplicity. The man approached the lady and greeted her with an appreciation note on the way she was helping old aged people. They conversed for about half an hour where they got to know each other and their families. The man was so interested in this lady that he neglected his family's beliefs and went on to marry this lady

The family had initial friction because they always saw a girl from their caste to enter their house. But, the lady understood the situation very well and continued to serve the family. One day, the father got sick and was admitted to the Hospital. The mother was too old to travel to the Hospital from home. The son and his wife did the work of taking the father to the Hospital and looking after him. The lady stayed with the father the whole night serving him with his requirements. She did the job so well that the father was really impressed. He realized that, even if they had got a girl from their caste, she would hardly serve with such compassion. The father was relieved from the Hospital and taken home. He narrated how his daughter in law took care of him while he was in the hospital and he had hardly seen anyone taking care with such compassion. The family was happy to see the camaraderie building within the family. The family accepted the lady with full heart and they agreed that they will look at things practically not limiting their beliefs to a few systems

Beliefs that are inherited are difficult to forego. Our Minds make these beliefs as important and to be considered in every situation. But, every situation or experience we have is a new one with added variables. Do we need to hold on to such beliefs when we have a constantly changing World outside?

6

A young lady had developed a lethargic morning routine. The moment she woke up, she would need a cup of tea. She would break her fast late in the morning close to noon time. She felt angry and frustrated in the mornings. She used to feel agitated with everyone around

The behavior would continue at the office till the time she would have lunch. The moment she ate her lunch, all the anxiety would reduce and she would feel nauseated. This schedule brought her uninvited healthcare problems. She couldn't attend to her work properly

She visited a nearby Doctor. The Doctor enquired on her daily routine. The Doctor knew what was wrong. He advised the lady to follow a daily schedule which he prescribed. The day she started practising the new schedule all her problems took a back seat. She was more open for the day and embraced people around. His work performance improved. She was a happy person

What was prescribed in the routine? To eat something within a short time of waking up. Habits are governed by the Mind. If we develop positive habits our Mind helps us continue such habits, the same goes with negative habits which get accelerated because of the ease of acquiring them. Our body needs to be taken care of to perform at the expected level. To take care of, we need to be aware of how the body functions. The mind controls the physical body. It is when we go completely off track, that we tend to lose the connection between the mind and the body

Mindfulness and being aware of what's happening within ourselves every moment helps us to take care of the body continuously. The awareness brings in a sense of deeper understanding of what needs to be done, which sometimes looks confusing, but our mind is the best friend to guide us in taking care of our body.

By being aware of the mind-body connection, we achieve a peace treaty between the two

7

The family was relatively big compared to the nuclear families around them in the City. The first generation and the third generation stayed in the same house. The grandparents were religiously orthodox while the kids would question every action. The middle generation, the parents to the kids were quite often found to be stuck between ideologies

Weekend arrived and the family wanted to go for an outing. The grandparents wanted to visit a temple on the outskirts of the city while the kids wanted to go for a movie which looked to question religion and its beliefs. The grandparents were trying to convince the kids to come along for the temple visit, counterside the kids were trying to take the grandparents along for the movie. The father to the kids planned it in such a way as to complete both the activities

They visited the temple. The kids were not very happy visiting the temple. They questioned the orthodoxy principles which were followed, which the first generation people were not able to answer, because they had blindly followed them. The kids found a very young priest at the temple. The priest, finding the kids uninterested, called upon them and started interacting with them. After some introductory notes, the priest asked why the kids looked dull and uninterested. The kids revealed their side of the coin. The priest smiled at them and took them around the temple for a casual walk. He explained the science behind every action at the temple. He also revealed that he was also a rebellious kid during his childhood who now was trying to understand the science behind the actions at spiritual places. He also played football with the kids at a ground adjoining the temple. The kids had their energy back and were quite enjoying it

The family then went on to watch the movie. The movie started with a note to those who believed in religious rituals which requested them to watch the movie with an open mind. The movie highlighted a rebellious person who didn't believe in religion. He would question the actions by religious institutions and had studied such actions from a layman's point of view. He also took up the job to educate people on making sense of such actions, which was well accepted in the society. The movie tried to bring in some basic reasoning to blind actions. The grandparents, though a little disturbed, realized the importance of not following beliefs blindly. From that day onwards, the family used to engage in debates questioning the 'WHY' of the actions that they did, which everyone enjoyed because they had started to experience things with an open mind

Our mind with stored information restricts us from exploration. Because exploration brings on new information which might challenge the information that the mind strongly holds firm. But, it is through exploration that we learn. And exploration

happens when we have an open mind. How do we have an open mind? By being aware of what our mind is getting us to do at this moment. Is the mind acting rationally? Or is it just trying to repeat the actions based on existing information?

Answering those questions requires us to be aware each moment, every moment. And when we answer those questions, is the moment we start learning

8

A young lady in her late twenties was in search of a person to get married to. The lady had her own list of qualities that the person needed to have in him. The search was on for more than a Year now, but the lady had not found a person who was according to the list

She got to know a person from one of her friends who was believed to fit into the qualities. She met the person and found him to fit all the points on her list. They started dating, they felt they were getting along well. Yet, the lady found the person to lack in some aspects. She, not having other options, was trying to make this opportunity work for her

Meanwhile her team had got a new person at the office. They had a team dinner where the lady interacted with the person for sometime, where she found him to be an ideal person for her. Now, she was confused. On one end, she was trying to make an earlier partnership work, while on the other there was a better person whom she could approach. She started to be in contact with both and made them wait till she was sure of the person with whom she wanted to be. Out of frustration, both of the male left her to be with herself. She lost both of them and was at square one

We are taught to seek happiness from the outside experiences, the people, and the environment around us. We are never taught to seek happiness from within. A person who is happy from within sees a perfect person in everyone around him/her. Because, he/she is happy from within. Insecurity arises when we are attached and dependent on the outside World for our happiness. Be it materialistic or caring, when we are dependent on the outside, we tend to be insecure. And it is our thoughts which make us feel insecure. The 'What if?' loop keeps playing on in the mind. Until we get out of this loop, the mind keeps making you weaker from within. How do we get out of the loop? Be aware of what your mind is telling and trying you to do.

Right Action follows when awareness prevails. Till then, we are in the mind's custody

Stories at Work

1

A grown up man, still unmarried, had seen an always agitated and frustrated mother through his childhood days. Seldom was there a day when there was no fighting between his father and mother. Humans, however hard they try to stay together, somehow their ego in the form of incessant thinking shows up in their behavior. The man had a troublesome childhood which shaped him to stay away from women as he grew up

He used to stay alone, trying to stay away from women everywhere outside. At work, he was part of a team which had women in majority. This made his communication with the team complicated.

There was a young lady, quite talkative, in his team. She was a person who smiled at every situation and took it positively. She had carefully observed the man's behavior at the team's interaction. She approached this man one afternoon and invited him for a coffee outside the office. She wanted to know what was troubling this man, who was quite young

They met at the coffee shop. The man's behavior showed that he was not comfortable with women. She tried to stay positive as she did with every situation. They had introductory notes discussing their family. The man hesitated talking about his childhood. The lady understood that there must be some problem related to his childhood. The lady took it slowly to help the man get out of the problem. They met several times outside the office till the day the man wept like a child in front of this lady remembering his childhood. The stuck emotions came out and the man felt quite relieved discussing his troubles with another person. The lady helped him come out of that situation. He was thankful to the woman who helped him knowing that he was uncomfortable with women

Over the course of time, the man behaved well with women. He started talking to women more often at the team discussion. The lady was quite helpful in the man's effort to return to being a well behaved person in the society. He started to open up to situations and people. He was a joyful person now, enjoying his life. He realized that negative experiences are true as long as they are broken by a strong positive experience. He was troubled by a woman's behavior in his childhood, he was also helped by another woman who stayed positive in every situation!

Only when we are aware of how our past experiences are affecting our present behavior, can we modify our behavior. Sometimes, it happens by an outside force or it sometimes happens with inner realization. The more aware we are about our thoughts, the better we behave and react to the present moment

Can you restrict the information that gets stored in your brain? The brain absorbs all experiences around you and invariably stores without any bias towards positive and negative experiences. Call it the superpower of the brain, it has this incredible ability to store every experience which happens around you. The mind relates to such experiences whenever a similar experience happens.

Does your mind act the same way?

2

Two friends had joined the same Company. They worked in the same team. The Company had the legacy of creating strong leaders who worked through every department in the Company. The team also had a Leader who came through this legacy. He exhibited a strong confidence and authority in his work. The two friends worked under this Leader

The Leader wanted his team members to also follow the legacy and excel working through every department. The team members were given the freedom to choose how and when they wanted to go through this. The two friends were also given the same choice

One of them quickly chose and informed the Leader of how and when he wanted to go through this experience. He wanted to go through this experience right this present moment. His friend wanted and took some time to decide about whether or how he wanted to do it

While his friend took up the task and continued to enjoy the experience, the other friend was in a dilemma. The dilemma made him go into a thinking circle which did not seem to end. But, his friend was happily experiencing the work. Both of them met after a week and discussed the new experience. One of them was ecstatic and in joy about the experience, the other one was stuck in thoughts. Clearly, the other one was dull and non energetic. His friend asked him to consult the Leader about his worries

Time went on but the worried friend did not consult anyone and was stuck in his own thoughts. A month had passed since his other friend started the process. The team Leader called upon the members to get to know the progress. While every team member had started, the only one left was this worried person. The Leader asked the

reason for his inaction. This team member did not have any answer and was yet stuck in his own thoughts

The Leader called upon this team member to his cabin. The particular person was frightened and seemed to be in another World altogether. Then he slowly started revealing how his thoughts never stopped to run. The Leader understood his problem and asked to just jump into the process. He monitored this person on a day to day basis and counseled to just work without thinking about the outcome.

The team member got into the flow. The work made his mind not to think. He started taking every day as an opportunity to give his best in whatever work was given to him. He started excelling in the process of going through various departments. The two friends met again over a weekend. They both had interesting talks about work. Importantly, both of them were happy and present in this moment

3

A young lady had recently joined a fast growing Company. She was very excited to use the knowledge she had acquired through her education towards the Company's growth. She came to the

Office everyday with exuberant energy to do good work

She joined a Team which worked on some important projects for the Company. Her boss saw the potential in her to contribute positively towards the Company's growth. She started working on an important project with the Team

The Team started to interact with the Leader on the progress of the project. Everyone in the Team started giving their view on how the work was proceeding. The Leader sensed some confusion in the opinion of the young lady. Although her opinions were related to the growth of the project, the opinions had some confusing proposals

The Leader called upon the young lady for a conversation. The Leader went about carefully learning about the Leadership abilities of the young lady during her education. The Leader came to know that the lady possessed excellent Leadership and initiative taking ability. She then learned about the work process of the lady in the Company. The Leader came to know that the lady asked for opinion and perspective of her work outcome with other Team members before implementing it. The Leader got to know where the problem was. The Leader asked the Lady to confidently listen to her own knowledge and experience when implementing her work

The Young lady listened to the Leader's advice and produced some excellent work which made the Project stand out in the Company. She also went on to become a Leader herself in the Company at a very young age

We always look to ascertain our Work from others. We are concerned about what other people think. We are seldom concerned about our own acceptance of ourselves. What we get when we ask others is perspectives. Perspective is unique for each and every individual which gets built by his/her experiences. So, each perspective is personal to each person. When we listen to perspectives and try to act according to them, the action will be ineffective because we are acting according to other's perspectives. It may or may not be effective for us

Instead, we have to learn to accept ourselves. We have to accept our knowledge, our physical existence and our Mental prowess to do good work. Each one of us has all the required ability to do excellent work. We just need to accept ourselves fully

4

A young man in his early thirties worked in the logistics department of a consumer goods Company. He was entrusted with the work of safe and timely dispatch of the goods. His team consisted of a lot of people whose work consisted of physical labor handling the goods.

The young man was always seen to tell his team that handling goods is an easy task. According to him, physical labor was an easy task. Due to this he always pressurised the labor to work effectively and take less time to load the goods. This lead to a heated atmosphere in the logistics department with many disgruntled laborers

During this time the maid at the young man's home left without any further notice. The young man was not able to find a maid for about a month's time. All of this time, the young man had to do all the chores at his home. The man was exhausted throughout the day because of this. The laborers in his department saw this and asked the reason for his lack of energy. The young man told the laborers about the situation at his home. The laborers asked the young man to put their physical activity in perspective with what he had to undergo at house

The young man realised the struggles that the laborers go through everyday. He realised that the struggles that he went through during this period was nothing compared to the struggles that the laborers go through everyday. He also realised that it is not fair for him to pressurise laborers for more struggle. He came up with a plan to

effectively utilise the labor effectively without stressing and draining their energy. The team was a happy unit now working hand in hand without stressing people

We seldom put ourselves in other's shoes and experience the troubles that one is going through. It is only when we experience the problems ourselves that we understand the plight of others. Without this experience, our human to human conversation remains incomplete. It is only when we truly understand the experiences of others that we can connect truly with others

5

The day had some important work to be done. The young professional woke up and started listening to songs. He kept on listening to the songs till he reached office. He opened his laptop and opened the spreadsheet to work on the financial metrics

The mind started humming the songs he had listened to till he reached office. He thought they would cease to be. But, the mind was busy humming the songs. He couldn't relate why the mind was trying to remember the songs when he tried to focus on the work. He tried to gulp a cup of coffee and chat with his friends for sometime to distract the mind. But, the mind saw pleasure in humming the songs

He took a small nap of half an hour to relax his mind. The mid looked to be fresh, but again after sometime songs were there! His boss called him to his cabin to ask about the work. He was anxious and nervous, not in a position to explain clearly.

Then the boss calmed him down and asked him to relate the problem. The professional narrated what he was going through

The boss asked him to stop worrying. He asked him to take deep breaths and watch the breath. The man did it for about fifteen minutes and lo, the mind had calmed down! He finished the work within the stipulated time and got to know the trick!

He learnt that day that the mind tries to remember your pleasurable moments and try to repeat them in thoughts to keep you engaged and give you a sense of joy

6

The appraisal day was approaching, and as usual the lady was quite excited. The lady had had a good Year at the company with a few interesting projects she had been part of. Everybody was talking about appraisals. Talks about how each senior rated the appraisal was doing the rounds

The lady had not maintained a close relationship with most of the seniors. She was concentrating on delivering her work, which she did on a regular basis. Yet, there were talks about seniors rating the appraisal based on the relationship they had with the juniors. The lady was tense as to how she will be rated. Thoughts of a bad appraisal were doing the rounds in her mind. She got stressed and could not concentrate on the work.

The appraisal day had arrived. The lady was unusually tense and stressed. She was sweating without any reason. This was her thoughts turning into fear and anxiety. The head of her department called her to her cabin. She discussed how the appraisal was done and how the points were attributed. The young lady was now sweating furiously. Seeing this, the Head gave her a glass of water and asked her to relax. She narrated the story of how she finds Employees behaving tense on appraisal days. The Head narrated a few hilarious contexts she had witnessed over the Years. The young lady laughed at the situation and relaxed now. The head of the department explained that there was no need to be tense. The appraisal was a method to get effective feedback and a way to learn.

The young lady got the appraisal in her hand and she had achieved excellent numbers in all categories. The head explained that appraisals were objective and there was no room for bias. The numbers reflected on the quality of work she had delivered, nothing else. The lady was quite elated and happy. She came out of the room and found her colleagues still talking about the same aspects of the appraisal system. She realized that talks are only the perspective of others. They are not factually right.

We often tend to take perspectives as reality. In reality, everything we talk about is just perspective. Perspectives are only turned real by verifying them objectively. We take hundreds of perspectives on a daily basis from all the things we interact with including the entertainment mediums that we indulge in. Are they all factually right?

Then how do we pick the right from wrong? By being aware. By being aware of the talks you absorb from around you. It is you who has to decide whether a perspective is factually right

7

The man was a senior executive handling an important department for a Corporate Company. He used to be quite busy throughout the day for the Company's work. He used to delegate his personal work to his assistant, who without any hesitation would complete all his personal works. The habit was set in. Most of the work that the assistant did was the boss's personal work. She had no objection till the time she got her monthly salary. Due to some personal obligations, the assistant had to leave her job. A new male candidate was appointed to the position. This person was quite strict in allocating time for the right work. Office work meant office work to him. He considered this to be important for his career growth.

The senior executive started delegating his personal work to the new candidate. The assistant did the work for a week thinking that the boss must have been too busy. When the delegation of personal work continued to the next week, the assistant went to the boss and questioned him on the work delegation. He mentioned that he viewed office work as purely professional which contributed towards the Company's progress and that he will not continue to waste his time on the boss's personal obligations. There was tension in between the two and it was seen in the work outcomes of both of them

The assistant, quite straight forward in his approach, approached the CEO to narrate the problem. In the meanwhile, the assistant had submitted a critical aspect which could help the Company grow. The CEO had also taken notice of the recommendation. The CEO understood his rationality. The CEO called upon the senior executive for a chat. The CEO explained to the senior executive that the perspective of the assistant was correct and he asked the senior executive to stop delegating personal work to the assistant and do it by himself in his free time. He also made him aware of the recent work that the assistant had done. The senior executive sat in the lounge and thought about it with his open mind. He realized that it had become a habit for him to view his assistant in such a situation. He never realized that anyone can have the ability to create real impact in whatever fields they are in

The boss called upon the assistant to have coffee at a nearby cafe. He apologized to him for the manner he treated him and told him that he had realized his mistake. The coming days, the Team did a fantastic job in contributing towards the growth of the Company which put them in the limelight

Quite often we take behavior and outcomes for granted. And it is the mind which creates the expectation based on previous experiences. It is only when such beliefs are challenged by a strong positive experience that the mind changes its stance. In such situations, the mind looks stupid for creating an illusion, but it is the way the mind works. It is only by knowing about it and being aware that you can guide your mind to immersive present moment work which drives inner joy

8

The phone rang while he was on his way to the office. The technology Company which the person worked for was about to close a big sale. This person, the VP was quite excited. With this sale, he would get a good chunk of money and promotion at his Company. He told it to his driver, who always wore a smile on his face. The driver was happy for the boss

The deal closed successfully with the assistance of the president. He got into the car for the drop to his home. He was quite excited but also looked exhausted. He asked the driver to take him to a nearby restaurant for some refreshments. The driver helped the president into the hotel. The president was extremely obese with all of the lifestyle diseases. He was not able to walk from the car to the restaurant, which he eventually did with the help of the driver. The driver was a fit person who looked very healthy.

The VP and the driver sat on a single table and had some refreshments. The driver's face always looked fresh with a smile. The president asked the driver what made him look so young and energetic. The driver's answer was a little confusing to the rich man. The driver said he loved living. Living was his most loved work everyday. He had a routine to take care of his body and mind. He said he enjoyed each moment of living his life

The executive was confused. Because he had never viewed his life that way. He had taken it for granted and acted as per his mind's guidance which was influenced by the people around him. He realized the profoundness and depth of what the driver told him. He realized that all his life he had forgotten the most important aspect in his life. And that was Living

The executive then onwards changed the whole perspective on how he was wading through his life. He made strong changes to his daily routine which made him respect Life more than everything else. He made major positive strides in correcting his health. He made more time for his family and friends. Life seemed to go through a flow now

9

Two women who had joined the same Company out of college had reached senior managerial positions. Each one of them handled one product each of the Company. But, each one of them had a different philosophy of work. While one believed in developing good relationships with people around, the other focused on her work and nothing else

Everyday, the woman who focused on her work would see the other woman talking to people in the office which looked like they had good relations. The work focused woman felt that people didn't behave the same way that they did with the other woman whenever she approached people for work related reasons. She started to feel the need to be treated the same way as the other woman. She started to approach people around her at work and would try to talk about random aspects, but in vain. People couldn't relate to her new approach

She started to feel inferior which affected her work. The look was clearly readable on her face. Seeing this, her boss called her to his cabin for a chat. He went about it in a structured way so as to not confront the problem on the face of it. After an hour of discussion about her personal and professional life, she came about to discuss the problem that she was facing. The boss listened to all of it with a smile on his face. The boss explained to her that there was no problem with her work style. Being a workaholic was welcome in the Company. He also explained to her about the different ways of work behavior and that it related to human behavior at the base. The Company respected both the work styles and measured them without any bias. The boss told her that in fact, the way she approached her work brought in more effectiveness than the other woman's approach. This made her relax. She was back to her core style the next day onwards

The mind creates illusory perception about the happenings around us. The mind tries to reason out every action happening around us and in what way it will affect us. Remember, this is all happening in the mind, but the outward reaction is seen in the body's behavior. The mind makes us do all unnecessary actions which are reasoned as right in an illusory World of the mind. A sense of competition and jealousy is the mind working on its tricks. While, factually there will be nothing to the effect, the mind creates its own problems for which it provides a solution itself! Quite mysterious, isn't it? Such is the power of the mind

How do we tackle this? By being aware. By knowing what is factually right at this moment. Just because one person is more accepted among people, does not mean the other person is inferior. Everyone has his own strengths which they should stick at. Do what you feel right. Not what others feel you should do!

10

It was 8am in the morning. The young executive had already reached office and started going about doing his work according to his schedule. This young executive had climbed up the corporate ladder within a very short period of time and was just one position down to his boss. This had made many people envious in the office

The Boss reached the office at 11am and saw that the work assigned to the young man was there on his desk. Jealousy started to creep in the boss' mind. He even kept a subordinate to keep checking on how this young man was able to complete the work within such a short duration of time. The boss even tried to disturb the young man's work by calling upon him for unscheduled meetings. This made the young man a little irritated. He approached the head of the department and narrated the situation. The head called upon the young man's boss for a discussion. The head got to know that the boss was anxious and jealous of the young man's progression.

The head revealed the work numbers and metrics which made the young man climb the ladder so fast. The numbers clearly said one thing about the young man. Focus and precision. He always stuck on to the schedule he created for the day and made sure he did justice to each piece of work that he did. The head subtly told the boss that he had forgotten about the core of his presence at the office. The boss followed the hint and was an early visitor at the office with clearly defined schedules. He even started to interact more frequently and did the work in synergy with the young man

The young man eventually jumped the ladder and became boss to his previous boss after a couple of Years. But, the previous boss had learned important lessons through these few Years and was on a higher performance trajectory himself

Jealousy is a mind full of unwanted thoughts. Thoughts of why somebody else should be in a better position than oneself. Such thoughts arise because the mind makes us forget our own strengths and starts observing others. The thoughts keep building up which makes us lose quality time. By the time we realise it, we would have lost a lot of time! An aware person knows his/her strengths and works on delivering work in proportion to those strengths

11

The Company had appointed a young person for the CEO post. The Company had been struggling for the past couple of Years in keeping the growth intact. The board members felt the Company needed someone who is energetic and comes with fresh perspective to drive growth

The employees of the Company were older compared to the CEO. The CEO started working.

He had scheduled meetings with all departments where he wanted to discuss with every person in the Team. The employees had not faced such a situation before, where they had a boss who was lower in age than them. They were hesitant to share information with the young boss. The CEO observed this behavior for a week, he realized what was the problem. He had joined this Company after turning around another Company which looked similar to what he was assigned to do now

The CEO assigned more time to get to know the employees and understand the problem on a deeper level. He met every person on the managerial cadre and held open discussions with people in the lower cadre. He used stories and experiences from his past to get along with the employees better. He made them believe that he was there as a trusted person to help them grow. Slowly the employees started to view the CEO as a friend who is there to help them. The CEO charted a plan to turn the business around to a growth path which was well supported by the employees.

Uncharted experiences create doubt within us. And it is the thoughts which the mind circulates that create the doubt. The mind tries to reason out the thoughts with the information available to it, that is stored in us. It is only when these thoughts are uprooted by a sweeping positive experience that the mind learns. Learning comes through understanding. Real understanding comes when we observe without any bias

Stories in the Society

1

It was a misty morning filled with dark gray clouds. It had rained heavily the previous night. The city had a bad traffic condition the previous night because of water clogging and power outage. Everyone returning from office work reached late to their home, tired and frustrated

The bad traffic condition continued the next day with traffic jams in most of the places. A young professional, in her early 30's started riding her car to the office. Within a short distance she got stuck in a traffic jam. She had to reach the office for a meeting within a stipulated time. She started honking in traffic jams like many other people do.

She was angry, frustrated thinking about the meeting, her getting late and all of that. She was hungry which made the situation worse. She started honking incessantly on the traffic

A small kid riding along with his father, next to her car told her that everyone stuck in the traffic jam is going through the same experience. He asked her to imagine what if everyone started honking incessantly and how stupid it would look because the traffic will move when it does. He gave her a bar of chocolate he had purchased which lowered her blood pressure. She thought about the advice the small kid gave and realized the unwanted effects that her current behavior would have on herself. Then, she started thinking in the present moment and messaged her boss about the condition she was stuck in and that she would be late. Her boss replied that he was also stuck in a traffic jam and would be late to the meeting. She then realized the unwanted experience she just went through!

Being in the present moment helps the mind to act! Not to think. If the lady had assessed the situation when she started from home and messaged her boss that there might be chances of getting late she would not have gone through all the stressful experience

Do you remember going through such an experience? What did you do? What would you do after reading the above story?

2

It was a chilly winter morning. The young lady visited the garden as usual for her jog and meditation

The garden had a temple. A young priest in his late twenties performed rituals as per the suggested guidelines. The lady had differing opinions about religion, although she believed in spirituality. She developed a sense of a negative image of the priest based on her values.

The day went on as usual. The lady had signed up for a spiritual discourse in the City. The discourse promised discussion on real life examples. When the lady witnessed the person disbursing the discourse, she was taken aback. It was the same priest from the temple. The session witnessed discussing real life problems and solutions. The lady asked the priest how he could discuss spirituality when he was a priest at the Temple. The priest understood the depth of the question. The priest said that he viewed serving at the Temple as serving the people. Religious rituals meant serving people to him. He saw God in every Human being. And hence, he had developed an affinity towards spirituality. The thoughts were in sync with what the lady believed by herself. From then on, everyday the lady visits the garden, she greets the priest and sits in the temple for meditation

The beliefs we develop are based on the memories and experiences we would have had. Naturally, they do not apply to all situations. The mind makes you apply them to all situations. The lady realized that her Mind had influenced her decision making

Do you relate to having gone through such an experience? What did you do then? After reading this small story, how would you have behaved?

3

A young professional was rushing to his office for an important meeting. The day had unusual traffic congestion. The professional was in a hurry to reach the office and was driving unusually fast that day.

There was a sudden red light at the traffic junction because of an ambulance passing by. The professional could not stop his car suddenly and went over to hit an old lady who was crossing the road. The lady fell unconscious. The professional didn't understand what to do. His mind was in a mess thinking about all the possible near future scenarios that would happen because of the accident he just got into. The prospect of him getting questioned by the police, him getting into a situation where the Company can fire him, all illusionistic situations.

Ten minutes had passed since the accident took place. The professional was still into an illusionary thinking mode. People started knocking his window asking him to get out and take the lady to a Hospital first. He did so, right in the nick of time. The lady was administered to a nearby Hospital where she underwent small treatment for the wounds

and the muscle pain because of the accident. The professional meanwhile thought about the situation alone with an open mind without any thoughts. He realized how stupid it was of him of staying dead still for ten minutes while the lady was unconscious rather than taking her to the Hospital. He realized he was a victim of an overthinking mind.

Once the lady was awake, he explained the whole situation to the lady. The lady understood his situation and forgave him, requesting him to be mindful of the next time around. The Police team was there, she requested them not to trouble the professional and that she was alright. The professional was thankful to the lady and they became friends forever.

From then on, the professional knows what he is currently doing and is strictly focused on the work on hand, no matter what, other than medical emergencies. He remains mindful of the day long of his mind and behavior

Have you gone through such situations earlier? What did you do then?

4

A young man was actively into social service. He was working with people to make urban dwelling spaces more livable by making them greener, cleaner and a place where people helped each other without any barriers. He was doing a good job with quite a good following. He got invited by an international institution working towards betterment of societies. He accepted the invite but he had never done a public speech in his life

Thoughts of whether he could deliver a public speech started to do the rounds in his mind. He started to watch videos of public speeches, which made his thoughts more stronger on the negative side. He was about to send a letter to the institution saying he won't be able to make it to the organized event when an old lady came to him to congratulate on the work he was doing. She told him that the work he was doing took a lot of courage especially in facing people and motivating them to do such work. The man thanked the old lady and she left. The man got thinking about what the old lady told him, that it took courage in motivating people. He realized that all of his work was in making people aware and motivating them towards helping each other. And that giving a public speech about his work was such a small part of his experience

He went to the event and delivered a strong story which moved people so much that many people came after the event to meet him and congratulate him on delivering a

moving speech. He went on to do more such speeches on larger scale which helped him to gather more momentum towards his work

Thoughts are thoughts. They are not reality. Thoughts sometimes create artificial reality within thoughts which look accomplished in themselves. But, totally virtual

5

A young professional in his early twenties had just got into professional work after finishing his education. He looked to stay away from the crowd and didn't interact much with colleagues. The Company he joined held a formal induction programme where thousands of students like him joined together. All the professionals were seated according to their names. The young man was joined by a lady beside him

The lady was very talkative and bold. She started interacting with the man on various topics including personal ones. The lady observed the hesitation to interact from the young man, although the man tried to talk as much as he could. She found out that something was troubling this man. After the induction, both of them got posted on the same project. Both of them felt good, because the man had not interacted with anybody of the opposite sex so closely before

Day after day the lady started interacting more with this man. She saw an effort towards breaking away from the shy behavior from the man. But, he looked anxious when they were joined by other people. She invited him to dinner on a weekend. The restaurant was a rooftop one, tranquil and quiet. The man enjoyed the place. The lady started to probe into what was troubling the man in his behavior. The man started sweating and looked anxious. The lady consoled him to be his friend and only wanted to help him come out of his troubles. The man revealed that he was troubled by other students during his schooling. The school had notorious students who took advantage of his shy behavior. The man told the lady that since then, he has hesitated to talk to people and to be in the crowd. The lady understood the situation very well

She started making small behavioral changes in the man by making him join small groups. Initially she included only one other person with the two of them and slowly she started increasing the number.

She explained the situation and the behavioral issue with her colleagues who joined to help the man. They used to go to quiet places where the man felt good. The lady and the other people who joined started appreciating the man's presence and spoke to him about the positivity they saw in him. This therapy started helping the man and slowly but steadily he started interacting with the whole team in his project. He even started to take courage to speak to strangers which he seldom did previously. All his fears had been driven away

Past experiences, especially those which make us anxious and fearful, are stored deep within our memory base in the brain. These thoughts often keep surfacing whenever there is an anxious moment faced by us. Slowly the Mind makes us withdraw from such situations which becomes a mainstream behavior. But, it isn't so. We are all equally capable of being socially active. But, the

Mind keeps reminding us of the past and keeps telling us to withdraw from such situations.

How can we look at escaping this loop? How aware are you?

6

The people of the city much awaited the event where a famous personality, a well known yogi was to speak. The day arrived and a young fellow organizing the event went to the airport to receive this yogi. The young man had vigour of his age. He was dressed formally with a good fitting suit. The yogi came out of the airport and approached the young man. The yogi was dressed in very simple clothes. A khadi shirt with full sleeves and a lungi. The talk was about the subject of controlling our minds in the digital age. The young man felt the appearance of the yogi to be hilarious and thought to himself what will such a simplistic yogi coming from a small village share words of wisdom. The young man invited the yogi to the car and they left from the airport to the event venue

During the drive, they shared introductory information. The young man introduced himself and his background. The yogi was in joy to meet this young fellow. The city had unusual traffic that day, because of the event. The young man started showing irregular behavior driving through the traffic. He started sweating, started playing loud music in the car and was yelling at other cars trying to pass by. The yogi sat there with a smile on his face as though he enjoyed what was happening. The young man curiously asked, what made him smile at such a stressful situation. The yogi told him that everyone around him was stuck in the same situation and it was the thoughts that were going on in the young man's mind that caused the stress. He asked him to take a few breaths and put a smile on his face. He asked the young man to see himself in the others around him and imagine how he would have behaved. The man realized the unwanted stress that his mind was causing. They reached the venue

The yogi narrated the story of the young man in his speech. The nature of the situation related so well to the audience that everyone learnt how to be mindful of the happenings around them. The young man always kept a smile on his face whatever the situation be. This made him go through any situation without the mind interfering

Outside experiences, other than physical ones, should not affect our mind and our behavior. But, we somehow get influenced by outside experiences, both positive and negative. While practically, the mind should embrace positive experiences more, the mind takes in negative experiences easily. This brings about unusual and unwanted behavior in us. It is only by being aware of our thoughts and behavior that we can correct them

7

A young man saw an old man everyday at the market. The old man wore a smile everyday. He used to stand there and just watch the actions of people around. He used to laugh hilariously sometimes. He used to greet people in the Morning, even the street vendors.

The young man was curious as to what brought the old man such joy from a crowded market. The young man approached the old man on a Sunday. He asked him what brought him such joy and happiness, while he usually tends to get frustrated going through the market.

The old man took the young man to an open cafe across the street for a coffee. The old man asked the young man to just observe the actions of people in the market. At first, the young man didn't observe anything. It was just normal boring things he observed. But, after some time his mind started to really observe. He observed the rat coming out of its hole to grab a piece of the vegetable near to it. He observed a woman arguing loudly with a vendor. He saw another person interacting with another vendor who was quite friendly. He started to observe every small action happening in the market. His mind was super active. He started to react to the situation in the market and felt how small these issues were. He became aware of his own irritation and how silly it was for him to feel that way

Pure present moment awareness makes you flow through yourself and your surroundings. Chaos and behavior of people around you will not affect you. You will just flow through the situations in a joyful state

8

A kid studying in early school wanted to pursue cricket. His father was a cricket fan and had played some first class cricket himself in his early years. The kid viewed his father as an inspiring figure

The kid approached the sports mentor at school. This sports mentor had an unusual selection programme. The programme started with understanding the body and mind of every individual through putting them through various exercises. The

programme, according to the mentor helped identify true talents in each kid, which was evident from his record

The sports mentor asked the kid to go through the programme, while the kid asserted to practice cricket. The programme revealed that the kid was fit to be a footballer rather than a cricketer. The mentor told this to the kid. The kid was sad that he cannot be a cricketer. He didn't interact properly with either the mentor or his father for a week. He was confused. The mentor visited the father and revealed the findings of the programme. The father, mature now, understood the perspective of the mentor. The father called upon the kid and discussed the matter in the presence of the mentor. He told the kid that he believed in the mentoring programme and he should believe too. He also told the kids that everyone has his/her true talents which should flow out.

The kid pursued football which later on he excelled in. He went on to become a national level footballer. The mentor was grateful that the kid and the father had an open mind and an intent to explore

The information fed into us in the early part of our life stays with us for the longest period of time. And the information coming from the people we relate closely becomes beliefs. Beliefs are hard to challenge, because the mind treats it to be true because it was true with the people we relate to. Beliefs within us restrict us from exploration. Exploration means learning. Learning of the self and how we interact with the surrounding. Through exploration, we learn new abilities and behaviors within us which help us towards a positive life. By being aware of what information is restricting us and how the mind is acting towards it, we will be in a position to challenge such action of the mind. Awareness creates that path towards learning and wisdom

Working of the mind - Information storage and effects

Do you really experience the things around you? Or do they pass by you in a hazy manner? Have you listened to the early morning chirping of the birds? Do you really interact with a baby when it comes to you, or is it just another passing by act for you? If you are present in the current moment in time, your senses tend to absorb the experiences completely. Your mind tends to absorb all the sounds, all the experiences happening around you. It is when your mind is engaged in the actions happening around you that the mind is relaxed. It tends to restrict me from getting into thinking mode. You can do this simple exercise. Go to a nearby park, sit and close your eyes and try to make your mind observe all the actions happening around you. People talking around you, the sounds of the steps of people walking closeby, the distant honking of an automobile, all the experiences happening. The mind can observe all the experiences simultaneously and tell you at what distance and at what frequency the sounds are coming from. Amazing isn't it? The mind is the most powerful tool you have! Isn't it a total waste when you use it for thinking unwanted thoughts? Think about it!

A major source of information coming into us is from the people whom you spend time with on a daily basis. Be it your colleagues, your family, your friends. Humans innately behave to influence. They tend to impose their perspective onto you. It is only natural. But, the mind absorbs each and everything that comes in and starts the thinking mode. You will start thinking about the effects of each of the information that gets in. You can relate here. See what your mind does when you pass through a crowded place. You will agree that the mind thinks and gives perspective of each and every thing you experience. Be it a person speaking aloud on the phone, or an old lady moving slowly or a baby happily smiling. The mind either reacts positively or negatively based on how these experiences relate to your memory. If a related experience shows up in your mind which has had a negative effect on you, your mind reacts negatively. There is a physiological effect to this. Your mind makes your nerves contract, releasing stress causing hormones which gobble up your energy. Now imagine how many of such experiences you go through on a daily basis. No wonder why stress is factfully the cause of the majority of lifestyle diseases these days. Are you following the narrative here?

Everything you experience around you, your mind has something to say about. And it is the information stored that the brain relates to, which makes you react the way you do. If an experience relates to a positive memory, you will react positively to such experience. Otherwise, you will be anxious and stressed.

Note that it is just your reaction based on the memory that is stored. It is not in reality based on facts. The mind and memory tricks you to react in a certain way which is just an illusion loop. Can you relate?

Most of the information that is stored in our brain comes from the experiences and the senses we go through around us. The people we interact with, the experiences we see and go through(both good and bad), and the entertainment channels we indulge ourselves in. But, the mind keeps those experiences in priority, which either would have a negative or a positive effect on you. You might remember a baby's smile which energised you positively or you might also remember a horrific accident which happened in front of you. The brain tries to put such experiences in priority, to be related to similar experiences you have later on life

Questioning is an integral part of learning. It is only when we question various aspects of how and why things work the way they are working currently, that we can understand the working of the self and the actions in surroundings in depth. A memory saturated mind, by logic tries to block this questioning because the information looks to be filled already. It is only when we bypass the mind and pretend that our mind is empty that we can learn. But, the mind is not empty, is it? It is by being aware of how the mind tries to use the information already stored to specific situations that we can explore to act in effective ways

Haven't you observed? Before you start any job, your mind tries to think about how you are going to do it. And if the action relates to a past experience, the mind tries to compare the two and make you think whether you are able to do the job or not. And this is all happening in the mind, not in reality!

Think about this. Do you need to think before calling another person? Another person is just like you. A Human Being doing his duty which can be related. Then why do we think about calling a person and fearing what will happen on the call? You just need to pick up the phone and talk. Random talks are the most remembered ones, because there is no outcome expected out of it. And it is the random calls that allow us to know the person more

Perspectives tend to build our behavior. The mind does not differentiate between a perspective and a fact. It keeps gobbling everything which has been conversed and stores it in your brain. The majority of the information which we attract from others are

just perspectives. What is right to one person may be wrong to another and vice versa. But, the mind supports your ego which creates tension between two individuals

Conditioning, as it is said of our minds, is the perspective in the form of information that gets stored in our brains. Right from the time we are born, we are fed perspectives. Perspectives on how to behave, what is right and what is wrong, and all those aspects which are related as to how we should conduct ourselves in society. Conditioning restricts exploration and learning as it restricts our action in situations which are governed by the perspectives that are fed previously

Conditioning is the beliefs which get stored into your memory base. They usually come from your interaction with the society. Beliefs are strongly related to people you hold closely with you. Your parents, friends, colleagues whom you respect and look upon. These are the points from which you consider information as beliefs. It is hard to break beliefs once they are formed. It is only when you keep your mind open to experiences without any expectations out of it that such beliefs get challenged and turned upside down sometimes. Learning happens with an open mind, not a restricted mind.

Thinking creates an illusionary world of activities which the mind conjures up as possible future outcomes. After all, the mind has the ability to reason various possibilities. But, these are all happening in the virtual world of your mind. The reality turns out to be quite different!

Do you remember a moment where your mind was completely empty? No thoughts, no remembering of past experiences, nothing. The mind is completely at peace with itself, flowing along with the experiences happening around. Monks who do continuous meditation are able to achieve this state. Their minds just flow with the experiences happening around, without getting disturbed by any of them. This state of mind allows for maximum involvement and learning from the experiences around you

Early Mornings are a good time to watch your mind's behavior. When you wake up, you will observe that the mind goes about looking for memories and experiences. You may find the mind singing a song, or remembering the football match you watched the previous night or some other experience. But, the mind tries to relate to some memory. Strange, but the mind tries to relate to the present moment with past memories. Some call this the protective behavior of the mind

The mind will also reason out why it is okay if you didn't wake up at the time the alarm bell went on. It tries to reason the way you intend it to. It is that initial effort from a

resting position to an active position that the body and mind do not fall in line. I believe most of you can relate to such an experience

By watching such behavior of the mind without any thoughts, just watching the thoughts will make you aware. And it is by being aware without any biases that you react in a rational way to it. It is only when you realize that your mind is making up reasons for not doing the physical activity, you can wake up and do it. It is when you are aware that your mind does not have anything interesting to get involved in, then it starts relating to stored memories

Experiences create an expectation of similar outcomes on future experiences. If it is a negative experience, the mind relates such experience to similar experiences you go through in a future time. In case of a positive experience, the mind relates to such an experience when you go through a similar positive experience in a future time

Negative experiences tend to stay with us for a comparatively longer period of time compared to positive experiences. Negative experiences tend to trigger strong electrical impulses in the brain which affect more than the positive experiences. A good example of this is a kid who has been troubled by his surrounding environment through his childhood. This makes the kid retreat from interacting with people around him which gets continued into adulthood too. We see many people hesitant to interact with people around them freely. Why do you think they act that way? The person near him is just another Human Being! It is the experiences which the mind relates to whenever he/she encounters such situations.

Thinking on purpose is a necessity. Thinking about how to effectively go about completing a project at the office requires thinking. Thinking about how best you can utilise your holiday season requires thinking. But, it is the art of not letting your mind drift away into other thoughts, that will help you make it effective

Are you aware of your surroundings? Are you aware of the baby crying across the street? Can you hear the distant horn from a manufacturing factory? Do you swiftly move across a crowded street? Or do you stand there clueless and frustrated?

Awareness of the present moment brings joy in chaos. You will enjoy chaotic situations because you are aware of yourself and your surroundings. You are aware of every small action happening around you, because your mind is completely involved in it. The moment you are not aware, your mind drifts into thoughts.

Action gives the impetus for the mind to focus on the act you are doing right at the present moment. Also, the mind has its own reasoning as to which work is important. Most often, when the action you are in at the present moment is not

important, the mind sets itself free into thoughts. It may be while you are traveling in a bus, or buying groceries at a local store, or waiting in a queue. Your mind starts to get into thoughts of the past, present and the future. For example, waiting in a line can make you frustrated and thoughts of anger and discomfort make rounds in the mind.

But, action is action. Whether you are walking across the street, or playing with a kid, action should make your mind concentrate on the present moment. Because, you need to be aware of yourself and your surroundings all the time! Imagine yourself crossing the street with your mind deep into unwanted thoughts. You will not be able to hear a nearby car honking at you and you may end up in an accident. Thoughts are addictive. Hence, action should ideally make your mind aware.

Action doesn't mean physical action. It can be meditation. Or you can ask what is the most important action that I do on a daily basis? Living! You live everyday. And it is the biggest part of the action you do in your lifetime. When you become aware of your living, there will be a huge transformation in yourself and how you view your surroundings. All of a sudden your mind gets super active and starts concentrating at a deeper level at everything you sense through the five senses. You will feel alive live never before

Such is the profoundness of the mind! Present moment awareness makes you flow through the day. Many people struggle through the day, mainly because of the effect of mind and thoughts. Present moment awareness of yourself alive brings in the profundity which makes you glide through your days with a smile on your face

Happiness comes from being mindful. The greatest reason for happiness should be that we are alive and in good health. But the mind with the influence from the society around you tends to prioritize ineffective meanings of happiness

Society often helps the mind to prioritize that which is not critical to Life. And "Living" is quite a demanding job. It needs disciplined action from oneself. Being mindful of our day to day behavior helps us to be aware of which tasks are important.

And it is the greatest source for Learning. Being mindful helps us to "Live"

What is Chaos

By definition, Chaos is confusion. A state where you won't understand what to do in a particular situation. The society at large refers to Chaos as situations where a large group of people are congregated. If we really understand the deeper meaning here, Chaos can arise from one individual too!

But, the truth is that Chaos starts from within us. How can Chaos arise out of a single person? It is the thoughts, isn't it? When your mind bombards multiple thoughts for a single situation, you will be in chaos as to what to do. Because the mind tries to reason why each thought can be right. In such a situation, you will be in complete confusion as to what to do. In such a situation many of us will skip and run away from the situation completely not understanding what to do

Chaos between a group of people is a classic situation to understand Human Behavior! Consider a small family of four arguing about a situation or a subject. Now, each one of them expects the others to behave and act according to their own beliefs. But, in reality, each one of them is acting according to his/her beliefs. Chaos or confusion arises when the mind of each one of them tries to reason that their line of reasoning holds true. It is a situation where the mind reasons out that our stand holds effective, not others. In reality, each one of us are victims of our informed minds with beliefs, which makes us not to view situations with an open mind. We cease to explore

Chaos in a large group of people is an extended version where a small group of people try to control the actions of a larger group of people. The minds at play become so big that situations often go haywire with each person acting according to how his/her mind is asking to act. Each one of them is doing the right thing according to them. But, it becomes a huge confusion to understand this behavior in a large group

Then, how do we control chaos? By being aware of how our mind is trying to reason for ourselves. Does the reasoning hold true logically and factfully? Is my Mind open to listen to other's points of view? Your mind will be bombarding the information stored within you as to check whether other's actions hold true. Being aware of this act of the mind and trying to have an open mind towards discussions can bring coherence in people

We have acquired the behavior of controlling others in their actions and behavior. But, if we truly understand how our minds work, we will be in a position to tactically flow through such situations and bring coherence between people. People management, remains to be one of the toughest behaviors, due to the complexity created by our Minds

It becomes easier when we understand the mind's play. Today's workplaces are much matured with factful reasoning methods. Yet, the mind's play will always be there, where it tries to reason otherwise. Having an understanding of the mind's actions can be handy at workplaces. It provides a base for smooth behavioral flow between employees and hence a productive work environment

Controlling the public becomes much tougher, because there are so many minds at play! How do we control chaos in such situations? There has to be a premeditated set of actions leading to a coherent behavior. This is why, Leaders who understand the role of mind in Human Behavior excel at top leadership positions in public life.

Needless to say, chaos and confusion drains a lot of energy and time of each one involved. Understanding and flowing through such situations brings in coherence and synergy between people. The exact opposite of chaos. The Mind is the master, isn't it?

Behavioral outcomes of a thinking mind

A thinking mind brings out undesired behavior in us. All such behavior creates friction in the flow of life. Valuable time gets lost in this effort of inaction which also ensures that our energy is lost. Let's look at some of these behaviors

Assumption

A thinking mind will assume certain actions both on the outside and the inside to happen as thought of. Outside here means the outside environment which includes other`living beings and other things which interact with us. Inside means our own actions. Assumption makes us lose quality time in inaction while the mind makes us feel that action has been taken. Assumption creates confusion which leads to other behavior like stress and fear, because the action would not have happened in reality

Assumption is caused by a thinking mind using the information that is stored in our brain. " He/she will act this way because other people have acted this way previously" ; "He/she would have acted like this" - the Mind tries to relate current Actions with previous instances. The Mind also assumes other's actions based on how you would have acted. The mind uses such information to every situation and justifies why such assumptions should be valid. Although there might be chances of the assumptions hitting the bullseye, these chances are very less. When assumptions turn to happen in reality, they are called fluke

Assumption is one of the major leakages to the quality time we have which can be utilized for productive use. This behavior will build upon the assumptions on many actions which result in complete inaction in reality. This has a bearing on our self respect and image too, where inaction leads to lessening of confidence.

How can this behavior be corrected? By acting based on facts and constantly interacting with both the inside and the outside. By being mindful of how our minds can drag us into this behavior, we can proactively act towards productive results

Fear and Anxiety

What is fear? I mean, by definition and in reality, fear is a behavior which drives us away from certain actions and the outside environment. Getting in front of a cobra

should make you fear because you know that a bite can bring death upon you. So, logically, we should fear only when such interactions happen

But, a thinking mind creates a virtual World where it makes us feel like the actions which might harm us are on play all the time. How does the mind do this? By thinking. Thinking about the outcome of our actions and playing its card of protective measures. The mind tries to answer the outcome of future actions based upon the information stored in the brain, which gets into a never ending loop of thoughts. The 'What If' clause keeps repeating and situations get added on to the loop which gets the mind to keep the loop operating

Fear is another major cause for inaction. We waste a lot of time thinking about the outcome of our actions rather than doing them. Fear also makes us feel less confident because of the inability to take action which gets compounded over time.

How to get this behavior corrected? Action combined with present moment awareness will help us correct this behavior. Being mindful of what our mind is thinking when we do certain activities can help us in learning how the mind works in those situations. This awareness combined with a strong intent to act is how we can defeat this behavior

Procrastination

This is one more behavior which is the result of a thinking mind. This is also an extended behavior of assumption. What is procrastination? In simple terms, procrastination is postponing work to a future time. Is there a need to put off some work to a later date? Scheduling work is different, in that you dedicate a particular time slot for work which typically gets done. But, procrastination is different. How does the mind work here?

Procrastination is a behavior where the mind reasons for putting off work for a later date. The mind creates its own virtual environment where it makes us believe that the work can be done at a later date also. Quite perplexing is it not? The mind uses thoughts coupled with the present information stored in the brain to reason that it is okay to get a certain work done at a later date. Slowly, this reasoning applies to all the work including the chore day-to-day work. The result is all work gets procrastinated and life looks like a stand still

This can bear serious negative effects on our behavior. One, our confidence in attempting to complete any work, even mundane jobs gets a dent. Two, the behavior gets compounded easily just like negative habits. This makes it difficult for the mind to get out of this behavior

How to reverse this behavior? By being purely aware of the moment. What is your mind thinking when you approach certain work? Does it try to reason out why you should not or cannot do that work? Is that reason justifiable? No! We live in a constantly moving World where action should happen in a flow! Keep watching your thoughts. That awareness will help us to keep acting in spite of the thoughts. When we do this continuously, the loop gets broken and the mind releases itself from the procrastination loop.

What are you doing now? Thinking or Acting?

Hatred & Animosity

Oftentimes it is our thinking mind which makes us hate another person which on an extreme level turns into animosity. Is there a reason to hate another person? Or can you give a legitimate reason to hate another person? Even if we give a reason, it will turn out to be very short term oriented

But, we tend to take it forward right? We mean, the hatred and animosity continues from the situation where it started. What is the reason for this continuity when that situation has long gone? It is our thinking mind. Whenever we are reminded of the particular person our mind remembers that one specific incident which caused discomfort. Does that behavior remain forever?

Ego is an extended form of this behavior where we categorise ourselves, most often to view ourselves as superior to others. The Mind helps us in reminding us of this behavior all the time. Ego, most often, gets us into a position where we neglect the Actions happening around us, where we stop learning. Jealousy is an extended part of this behavior where the Mind starts questioning the superiority of others over us

We live in a fluidic World where Action is taking place all the time. The mind keeps us in the past when everything around us keeps moving! Who gets troubled by this behavior? Ourselves! We tend to run in the loop created by our minds which restricts us from flowing in the stream of action surrounding us

How to get out of the loop? By being present in the moment. By being mindful of what our mind is dragging us to do. Awareness creates a ground for the mind to realise its own actions and to judge how far they are effective in this moment

Depression

Depressed in simple words means to be lowered to an inactive position. What happens when a person is depressed? He/she tends to lose interest in life. By life, we mean ourselves, the surroundings and the actions happening around. Why does this happen? Because the mind relates a particular situation/experience to every action inside and around us. The mind drags us into an infinite loop of thoughts which are reasoned towards keeping the situation as it is

Quite complex, is it not? Depression is a major psychological disorder that we face today! But, is it so complex? It is not! Only if we understand the basics of how our minds work! Of course, it takes a lot of determination to break the loop of thoughts, but awareness of how our mind is helping the behavior to stay is much more important

How do we break this loop of thoughts? By being aware! By being aware that an experience which has happened in the past does not stand true in a continuously fluid environment around us. By being aware in the present moment, how our mind is influencing us to get into that behavior. We just have to be an unbiased observer to the actions of our mind. This awareness helps us take effective actions in the present moment

All of the above behavioral outcomes drain out energy from us in the form of stress. You must have observed incessant sweating when you are involved in such behavior. These behaviors cause the body to lose vital energy which is required to conduct ourselves in an effective manner on a day to day basis. So, the loop gets extended to physical behavior which again gets repeated. If such behaviors continue for a longer period of time, they tend to restrict us from living. The basic and most important Action there is!

Awareness and being completely present in the moment helps us get into an effective action mode. Awareness of the thoughts, how the mind is utilising the thoughts, how the body is reacting all of these awareness creates an impetus for fluidic motion. By fluidic motion, we mean getting into the flow of actions happening around us without any restrictions

Can we restrict information flow

You must have observed that your mind tries to relate to your memories. It may be that the mind tries to get into a survival mode, because an empty mind would mean that all that you have done till now in your life went for waste and you are starting afresh. The mind tries to relate your existence to a deeper meaning. And it is the memories and information that the mind recollects in doing so. Quite often it is the thoughts of fear and doubt which surface easily, because of the psychological impact that such experiences have. So, you are again in that loop! And this is happening first thing in the morning when you wake up

What is chaos? Chaos, in layman terms is the noise from the surroundings coming at you, which you are not able to handle. Chaos, by logic, looks unorganised. The in numerous sources of information flow towards you, makes the mind confused as to which one to focus on

Present moment awareness helps the mind to be aware of every action within you and outside, which makes it easier for the mind to create a flow to the information coming at you. The flow makes the mind to observe the information without disturbing the flow of the information

How do you get out of the loop and into an action mode? Take a deep breath, be aware of the thoughts and smile at them. Then get into action mode with your daily activity being aware of the thoughts. You will observe that the thoughts will fade away

Your five senses keep registering information into your brain's storage hub. They do not differentiate between positive and negative experiences. But, the extreme experiences on both sides of the scale get registered at a higher impact scale.

A pungent smell will trigger your neurons and make them active. A sweet aroma which brings in positivity triggers positivity. A fatal accident which you would have seen would be registered strongly. The mind keeps registering all the information that your senses take in without any bias. But, it is those senses which trigger either a strong positive or negative experiences that get registered on a higher scale

And it is these strong experiences which the mind relates to whenever a similar experience happens with you. Call it the reasoning power or protective aspect of the mind, the mind keeps relating to the information. And most of the time, the mind will get into a loop of thoughts. It is at this moment, by being aware that you can get out of that loop

By being aware of what your mind is doing and your surroundings that you can get into the present moment filled with action

A Baby's example

Have you noticed the fearlessness and the excitement with which a baby goes about experiencing the environment outside of her? Completely fearless! Be it approaching a dog, going to the balcony of a 50th floor without having any fear, whatever it is that we grown ups would think before acting, the baby acts before thinking! Why? The baby doesn't know the outcomes. The baby doesn't know that a dog might bite, or a glass might break. Of course these are very simple examples. But, you can see the cause and effect relationship here. It is the knowledge about the harm that some actions might cause, which restricts adults from taking action in certain instances. As the baby grows up and gets to know about the outcome of actions, the brain instinctively helps before such actions. Instinct comes through experiences. The mind learns that a snake can harm you if you touch it through experience. Or through knowledge. But, better learning happens through experience. Hence, we slowly learn to learn about good and bad things, although it is just a perspective.

But, it is the over thinking about the effects through thoughts which make things worse as we grow up. The people around you, society aids the mind's behavior in this. The surrounding environment keeps feeding information about what is good and what is bad continuously. The mind keeps storing this information. Whenever such an experience is approached, the mind goes into relating to the information stored which relates to such an action. Let's consider a very simple example here. You are about to go for a road trip on your bike and you know that you ride a bike pretty well. One of your friends cautions you about a tragic and horrific accident which had happened a couple of weeks back on the route you are planning to take. Another friend relates an enticing experience he had had when he drove down that route. Now, your mind starts to think. Which one to believe? The mind incessantly starts thinking about the future actions which might happen, although all are self created illusions of the mind. This happens, even after you know that you ride safe and responsibly! Why does this happen? What do you do? Take the risk or not? It is for you to decide. Do you believe in yourself?

As we grow old, we absorb experiences around us which get stored in the brain. Everything you experience, people talking, bird chirping sounds, music you listen to, the movies you watch everything gets stored. Although, the mind stresses on those experiences which are extreme. Either a hilarious movie or a tragic experience. The mind stores these information as critical points in the experience history. It is strange as to why your mind stores different information differently.

Maybe it is the protective instinct that works here. It is this information availability and experiences that hold us back! We tend to think before acting. I will agree to your doubts here that some thinking has to be done. Thinking on purpose or towards a goal does not affect your mind. But, remember work happens by Action

A Monk's example

You may have often observed monks do not react in the typical way to outside happenings. Be it going around a busy market, or witnessing an accident, or witnessing some stressful situations. They usually have a smile on their face all the time. Do they selectively absorb information from the experiences? Or is their mind unaffected?

The mind remains the same! But, it is sheer presence in the moment which makes the difference. Monks are super aware. They derive this skill through constant meditation for long hours on a daily basis. Do they get disturbed by a fly sitting on their nose while they meditate? You bet!

It is by observing their mind's reactions and thoughts that they remain unaffected by experiences around them. They understand that the mind's effort to relate happenings around them to the information stored is not effective, because the present is present, not past or future. And it is by being present in the moment that we can enjoy the moment

Monks are super mindful of themselves and the surroundings. They are aware of their physical body and their mind while also being super aware of the happenings around them. Hence, they do not react to situations in the usual manner that a normal person does

Pure present moment awareness allows you to flow through time. Not create friction and lose energy. We are talking about energy here, quite interesting isn't it? Energy is limited on a daily basis. Your physical body needs energy to do basic physical work, so does your brain to perform intellectually. Now, when we create friction to the flow, we lose valuable energy. And hence, do not do justice to the action happening in this moment

We can achieve a flow by being mindful. By being happily present in the moment. Present moment awareness brings in a sweet joy towards life which makes you go through situations in pure joy

Action - The sword against thoughts

Have you observed how fast time flies when you are occupied in a work which you enjoy? A musician playing his music is seldom troubled by thoughts, a baby's astonishment at everything she observes is such a jewel act, a monk's act of LIVING helps him flow through life without getting troubled by unwanted thinking

One aspect that we have written quite often in this book is that the mind tries to keep the brain busy. If you are not involved and focused on the current action, your mind will wade into thoughts. You may ask whether only the work you love to do prevents you from getting into the thoughts world. For starters, passionate work does look to provide that pathway. But, look at the Monk's example. A monk makes Living as his most important and passionate work! Hence, he doesn't get troubled at any point in his life!

What activity absorbs the majority of the time in your life? Living! Isn't it? Our basic duty is to live! But, hardly any of you would have viewed your life from this perspective. You may ask how to make living the most important activity? By being mindful of yourself and the surroundings. By being purely aware of your physical body and your mental conditioning while also being equally aware of the actions happening around you. When you start observing the actions around you to the minute details you will start to appreciate the depth of life. Both yours and your surroundings. It is when your mindfulness reaches such a stage where you witness every action in depth with joy, that you will achieve a flow state

Training our Minds to focus on one single Act for a long period of time is a sure pathway to help the Mind in not getting distracted into thoughts. What happens when we do this, while thoughts will still be there, they will appear and end in a flow manner while we continuously focus on a single work. The Mind partially observes the emergence of such thoughts and since we are concentrating on one single Act, the Mind realises that they are unnecessary. This continuous realisation from the Mind makes it learn about the disturbing nature of thoughts, which is then carried on in a positive loop. For sure, Living is that continuous Action which we can focus on, no matter what other work we are doing

So, Action does not necessarily mean a particular important work. Action means being purely present in this moment. Pure present moment awareness brings in a joy that clears all the divisions that a conditioned mind creates. A new level of consciousness gets created which keeps your mind active and in a joyful state

Can we wipe out information to be mindful

We have tried to link information storage to thoughts and how it restricts us from learning. We narrated a baby's example previously to give a perspective of how the mind works without any information being stored. All kinds of unwanted behavior like Fear, Jealousy, Insecurity tends to go away when there is no information stored. Zero information about the mind equals the brain. Pure intellect at play!

We may ask, can we erase the information stored so that we can start afresh in being mindful? Or, can we selectively erase information stored in us, which will help us in being mindful? Sounds like a fictional movie scene! Doesn't it!

Our brain learns how to navigate in this World by information. Information serves as a base against which the brain tries to reason. Information also serves us in being protected from harmful situations. Information serves as a good base against which we can learn. Zero information means we will have to learn everything from zero state, which will gobble up a quarter of our lifetime, given the pace with which we learn.

So, how do we navigate through this maze? Awareness helps in understanding what information is stored in our mind. Of course, it comes through gradual experiences. But, we can be aware of the width and depth of information stored in us. This awareness creates the same effect of having a fresh mind. Awareness helps us in experiencing things from a fresh perspective.

So, we cannot wipe information from our mind. Yet, we can act like there is no information stored, which deepens the learning and understanding of self and surroundings

Mind-Body coordination

We have talked about how the mind works in the areas of storing information from experiences and your senses. Can we say that the mind controls the body? By controlling the body we mean controlling the free action of the body. It definitely looks like that!

Each of our actions is governed by the mind. The mind has its own opinion based upon the information stored. This action starts from the time you wake up in the morning till the time you go to sleep. The moment you wake up, you must have observed that the mind tries to recollect the information in the form of memories about recent happenings. It is the protective instinct of the mind which suddenly gets into reality from a partially dead sleep state. The mind tries to relate your existence and current circumstances to the information stored within you. In this way the mind tries to reason out your existence in your current surroundings. As you go through the day, you experience new actions from your surroundings which the mind, while relating to the information, absorbs these experiences irrespective of how they impacted your mind. The visual and hearing senses are the major contributors to the information stored because they can sense on a wider and deeper scale.

The mind tries to reason every action of ours based on the information stored within us which would have come from past experiences. This starts from the time you wake up. Imagine you have set up a time to wake up, the moment the alarm rings, the mind starts reasoning out why it is okay for you to sleep for some more time based on the information you have collected previously. Like this every action of ours is affected by the mind which reasons as to why and how we should act.

You can clearly see that the mind is trying to refer to information in the past. We mean here that the mind doesn't act in the continuity of the change happening continuously around us. This looks like a never ending loop where we are always behind on acting according to the present circumstances! We can see a lot of behavioral confusions because of this. The most important aspect that hurts in this act is the loss of time in bridging the gap between the past and the present. By the time we adjust to the continuous changes around us, a new day would have arrived!

Looking at all of this, it looks like not having the mind is a good option! But, the mind also helps us in staying relevant to our existence today from our past experiences. Then how do we tackle this issue, you might question?

All we can do is to be aware of how our mind is trying to influence each of our actions. Is the mind reasoning based on past experiences and information which are not valid in the present because of a continuous changing surroundings? This question puts us into a fix, isn't it? Because the mind always reasons from the past information! Then how do we solve this puzzle?

Again the answer is being aware! We have to be completely and deeply present in the present moment and also of how our mind is trying to influence. Awareness brings continuous understanding. Awareness coupled with understanding guides us in acting in the present moment in spite of the mind trying to influence. Because we are aware of the continuous changing flux. This awareness is the key to acting and making decisions in the present moment. This brings a renewed awareness where the mind and body tend to act in complete coherence. All of our actions tend to pass in the flow without looking tedious or disturbing. Be it professional work, actions at home or in the society, all of our actions tend to flow through the situations.

Real joy is experienced when there is coherence between the mind and the body. Because we are part of the flow, we become part of the motion around us without any resistance

Modulating the Mind in Body expressions

How do you come to know what is happening in your body? Suppose you are experiencing pain in some part of your body. How do you get to know about it? Through the signals sent to your brain. This is basic science. Does it end there? I mean, once you are aware, does it end there? Logically, the awareness and a small treatment either through a massage or medication whatever is suited should end that pain there

But, we observe that continuous pain in the same areas tends to get aggravated over time. Sometimes, it becomes so aggravated that medications do not help. Is there a psychological pathway leading to this? Of course, we are not trying to analyse from a physician's point of view here. We are just trying to understand whether it is only a bodily expression or if there is something which aggravates it

If we clearly observe, the brain activates the mind to focus on the pain area. Call it the protective mechanism of the Human Body. The mind gets super focused on the particular troublesome area. Now, when such episodes start happening frequently, the Mind starts playing its role. The mind will make us remember the previous instances and compare it with the current instance. Through this, the mind gets us into thinking mode. A thinking mode where the mind tries to enter a loop of causality and effects which makes the situation aggravated. The mind stresses the brain about the situation, which makes the loop complicated.

With increase in frequency of such instances, the mind will initiate behaviors like fear, anxiety, stress and other negative behaviors through the thinking mode. These behaviors increase in intensity with increased frequencies of such instances

This behavior is related to all other body expressions. The brain has the ability to identify and tell us where the problem is. But, the mind makes situation worse by bringing in related past experiences

So, the question to ask here is whether we can modulate the mind's behavior to reduce such unnecessary situations? Apparently such situations drain a lot of energy from us! So, it is important to understand whether we can modulate the mind's behavior in such aspects.

So, what can we do? The mind continues to absorb information and keeps relating to such information. The only way we can reduce such unwanted behavior is by being aware. Being aware of how the mind makes the body get into a stressful mode when such similar instances happen. We have to be aware that the body is sending signals to the brain that certain part of our body needs to be taken care of

This awareness helps us to bypass the thinking mind and get into action mode. When we get into action mode, we focus on how to reduce the trouble rather than thinking about past experiences. This awareness brings a deeper understanding of how the body works and how we can control it

We are also talking about the power of positivity here. When we are experiencing troublesome situations, most of the time it is the mind that is making it worse, other than deep troubling bodily ailments. By being super aware of our inner selves and telling the mind that we are doing good makes the mind not to go into loops of negative thinking. What happens overtime is we enter a state where the awareness itself will bring relief to some of the troubles

As philosophers and monks say it, on the inside lies the answers!

Awareness creates Freedom of Mind

Freedom is the ultimate need for living beings including humans, isn't it? Freedom to act on our own. Each one of us is unique and creative. It is this infinite potential in each one of us which makes us look for freedom. The basic necessity comes from this immense potential in each one of us

The Mind controls our Actions. Through the combination of stored information and thoughts, the Mind makes us do what feels right, which is not factually right in reality most of the time. We have said previously that we tend to be running in a loop of information which is in the past, because we live in continuous changing environment

So, when we talk of Freedom, how can we achieve Freedom of Mind here? Considering how the Mind works, how can we achieve Freedom from this continuous loop of information and thoughts? We would also like to point towards the beliefs and perspectives that the Mind gathers from others which tend to block the Mind from exploration and learning.

What is Freedom of Mind, we may ask here. Freedom of Mind is having our minds free of information and the resulting influences in our day to day Living. Freedom has the ability to help us take Actions according to the present moment, not based on past information. How can we achieve that when we live in an information age where we are continuously bombarded with information?

We have said previously that wiping out information from our Mind is not possible. Then, how do we break away from this continuous loop?

Continuous awareness of ourselves and the surroundings can help us take Actions in the present moment according to the changing interactive dynamics between us and the outside World. Awareness starts from within. We have to be aware of what our Mind is influencing us to do and continuously ask whether such Action would be right in the present moment.

Awareness helps us to continuously observe the changing nature of the dynamic interaction we have with the outside World. Awareness helps us to logically act according to the present moment and do justice to the current Action

When we are continuously aware, we create a path to Freedom of the Mind. We start on the path of remaining free of the influences of the Mind in our Actions. We become part of the fluidic motion around us and we flow along with it

Freedom of Mind helps us enjoy Living. As we have said Living is the most important Action for all of us

Physical Work as Therapy

Have you observed what happens when you carry out some physical work in the morning right after you wake up? Be it going for a jog, a walk, doing yoga or heading to the gym. The mind gets focused on that work fully without distractions. The mind watches your steps while you walk, your speed while you jog, the stress in the joints when you do yoga and the pressure being put on the body in the gym

The mind tries to learn how our body is responding to external stimulation.What parts of the body get stressed more, what parts of the body are struggling, the mind observes every aspect and makes us aware of the body. Quite amazing, isn't it?

Is there a correlation between physical work and mindfulness? It definitely looks like that! Although the mind sometimes tries to go into thoughts trying to compare our previous such instances with the current happening. But, physical work does look like a good therapy to bring the mind to be aware

But, is it possible to be physically involved all day long? We live in a knowledge economy where we spend most of the time on a desk, sitting. If you have observed, some of the best conversations happen when we are standing or walking. Have you observed it? If not, you should try it while you are talking on the phone. You tend to converse smoothly with the other person

Why do you think this happens? Because the mind is focused on your body. When we stand or walk, the mind gets focused on the body and our actions. So, when we talk while standing or walking, we are focused on that work, not anything else. This is why, if you have observed, when you stand and work, you tend to be focused more

Complete awareness of the present moment and achieving the flow state should be our goal. We are presenting pathways to achieve this state here, by relating how the mind gets focused when we are physically involved in a work

Deep breathing as a therapy

If you refer to scientific literature, the animals which live the longest breathe a few times in a minute. The breathing rate of humans is much higher than the tortoise. The tortoise is one of the animals which lives for the longest period of time. Yes, we are trying to link healthy living to breathing here

Tortoise, apart from being labelled as a slow moving animal, breathes very few times in a minute and is one of the few animals living for a longer period of time. We might all remember the story of the bunny & the tortoise and the learnings from it. Well, in the context that we are talking about here, it does look like the learnings hold firmly

But, there are other aspects related to breathing here. Have you observed that your breathing rate goes up when you feel behaviors like fear, anxiety, stress etc? These situations are a classic example of the mind affecting body behaviors. The mind brings out such behaviors in both physically and mentally stressful situations

Deep breathing aids us in the act of being completely aware in the present moment. If we logically see it, it is the nature of relativity that looks like acting here. While surrounding actions look like to be moving faster and creating friction, the nature of deep breathing tends to help us view each of the outer actions slowly yet deeply despite the fact that they are moving at their speed

This helps us to act with a deep understanding of the moving flux around us. Flowing through Chaos sounds like a good fit for such a state. We tend to understand situations deeply before acting which tends to bring an inner joy

We are not getting into the practicalities of how to breathe deep here. For those of you interested, there are innumerous sources from which you can learn. We have experienced the effects of deep breathing and we believe that it is beneficial in helping us reduce the mind's tricks

Monks and Yogis, by our understanding, practice deep breathing. And we know how calm they are in any kind of situation. It is the ability to look at every aspect of surrounding actions deeply that they tend to stay calm

Deep breathing augurs our ability to be aware in the present moment no matter what the situation is. When we achieve such a state, we tend to flow through situations without resisting or creating friction. This brings a state of inner peace where we are happy by ourselves

Living as the most important Action in Life

We seldom understand the true meaning of words. What is Life? Life in true essence means to live in completeness. What does living in completeness mean? It means being completely aware of yourself. Being aware of how your physical body is performing and your mental apparatus is working.

We know this is difficult to grasp, because of the various conditionings that we go through since the time we are born. We are taught everything apart from the basics. Quite startling isn't it? We are seldom taught of the "WHY" of our existence. It is the conditioning coming from various sources around us combined with the Human behavior that makes us appreciate superficial aspects of life than the basics of it

When you start being mindful, you will start realizing the true meaning of everything we do and interact. Mindfulness brings in that consciousness which helps us view the activities and experiences around us without being influenced by our conditioned minds. When we start doing this continuously, we reach the base of our existence. What is that base? Our life is to live. To live completely. Living completely comes from pure present moment awareness each day, every day.

Awareness helps us in seeing the reality behind the beliefs and perspectives which we absorb continuously from our surroundings. Most of the beliefs and perspectives, if looked at from the awareness lens, do not make sense for many of us because we are unique in ourselves. Awareness helps us to question such beliefs and perspectives which creates a doorway to learning, both for us and others. It is by being aware that we can achieve freedom of the mind, which is the ultimate need for each one of us. When the mind is free, despite the information being there, we start to live in the moment, opening the door for learning. It is when the mind is free that it can learn what is important and what not

It is then that LIVING becomes the most important ACTION of your life. It is then that we start to appreciate everything around us in full. You will be able to observe a fly as a living being doing its work rather than troubling people, you will be able to understand human behavior around you in depth, you will be able to notice each and every action around you in depth which brings in a godly wisdom in us.

When we embrace Living as a continuous and important action, we start to control situations which used to go out of control. The situations arising out of the typical human behavior and interactions where expectations get situations out of control. When we embrace Living, which is larger than any of our other priorities, we get over unnecessary trouble with ease

When we are graceful towards Living, all other needs and wants become secondary. This builds deeper meaning to our day-to-day activities and behavior which helps us towards being joyful from the inside

What happens by this, is that it creates a flow where in every action tends to fit in the flow without friction, because of the deeper understanding that it creates. Hence, life becomes a flow where you find yourself smiling all the time. Such is the profundity of mindfulness living

Flow to Life

Flow represents motion. Motion represents Action. So, when we refer to a flow state, we refer to a passionate and indulging Action which is not interrupted by anything. How can Life be interpreted as a flow state?

Continuous mindfulness brings about a state of pure present moment awareness. This pure present moment awareness helps you to observe every action within yourself and in your surroundings in depth and with the understanding of the true meaning of these actions happening around you.

When this happens, the mind absorbs every experience in its true essence and passes it on without getting affected hence not storing it into your database, because it is in continuous Action of absorbing such experiences from within and outside. When we reach such a stage, the mind is in a flow.

You will be in pure joy of living in a flow state. No experience, good or bad, will affect you from being in that flow. Such flow state creates a fertile field for us to grow, because we tend to understand things at their basic level yet deeply

Continuous awareness makes us part of the movement within us and around. Without any friction, we start seeing ourselves as part of the continuous movement around us. When we see ourselves as part of the whole movement, we continue to appreciate the movement despite the differences. Flow makes us to synergise ourselves into the movement which improves communication between fellow beings

Flow state helps us to develop a healthy mind with a healthy body, because it is the mind which controls the body. Flow state brings in the joy of Living. Flow state helps us in staying calm in chaos

Love towards Self and the Surroundings

Being aware in the present moment helps us to understand the deeper meaning of the actions by ourselves and others around us. Not only human beings, but all the living beings around us. Pure present moment awareness helps us understand that the majority of the unnecessary actions happening from us and in our surroundings are the result of the mind's tricks

It is this understanding that helps us to view every action happening from a compassionate angle. Such understanding helps us feel through the problems lying at the base of such experiences which makes us feel compassionate towards the living beings going through a particular situation

Compassion generates love towards others. Because, at the base of Living is Love. Living beings are Loving beings. By love, we do not mean bodily attraction or lust. It is that deeper wanting to care which comes from deeper understanding. To care is to love. Pure caring comes when we understand ourselves and others in true essence

Pure present moment awareness creates the flow state which helps us love and care for others around us. Because it is only when we are completely aware of ourselves and the surroundings in every moment that we can be in an action mode yet compassionate in our approach

It is by being mindful, that we can all solve the majority of the problems around us. It is our minds which creates the majority of the problems around us. Caring and Love is the true outcome of being mindful

The Healing Power of Love

It is a thinking mind which creates barriers and problems which look unnecessary. Thinking mind has created wars around us, divisions on the basis of religion and caste, geographical barriers and on and on. At the base of all barriers is a mind which is thinking, which also generates its own reasoning as to why it is correct in thinking and doing so

But, mindfulness and pure present moment awareness helps us generate a compassionate view for such actions. Because, there is in depth and complete understanding of every action within and outside. Understanding brings in compassion

It is compassion which helps us generate caring behavior for ourselves and other living beings surrounding us. It is from such a viewpoint, that we can influence others to view their actions and behavior in a mindful way. Positivity is a strong influence

Love is and should be the most desired outcome of being mindful. It is through Love that we can solve barriers and problems around us. It is through respect and equality that we can create a joyful Living. It is through joy that Living gets its true meaning

Love is the most potent cure for all Human related problems. A simple gesture of care has the ability to motivate a person to come out of problems, including diseases which sometimes do not get cured by medications. With the growing use of technology, we are seeing lesser human to human interaction, which is the need of the hour!

We Humans are vulnerable by ourselves. We are not strong enough to brave through the physical and mental pressure that we experience day-today. We are definitely capable of it, but we do not have the courage to be brave through Life alone. We keep searching for people who can understand us and care for us. Compassion builds that base where we Love who we are! When we do that, everyone around us looks like a friend, because we see ourselves in others. When this happens, the emergence of unnecessary behaviors which create tension, tends to fade away. There will be a sense of appreciation for every human being around us. When we reach such a state, we can say that true Love exists!

We may take examples of the likes of Mother Teresa, who selflessly helped people around without seeing any differences between any of them. Such a state requires deep compassion in action, which can come from a deep state of mindfulness

Mindfulness creates compassion towards self. For you to love your surroundings, you have to love yourself first. Mindfulness generates compassion and love towards self irrespective of your outward appearance, for it is the inner joy that matters to be in a joyful state. Only when we love ourselves can we view our surroundings with compassion and deeper understanding.

IN LIVING IS THE JOY. IN LIVING IS THE LOVE. LIVE FOR TODAY. LOVE FOR TODAY

Practical guide to be present in the moment

We have illustrated what mindfulness is through various stories till now. But how do we go about being mindful? That too in a world which has more distractions to offer you?

As we have said before Action acts as a sword against thoughts. We have also said that Living is the single most important action. What action does Living entail? Living for all living beings involves breathing as an indispensable action. We have to breathe to live. So, breathing is the action that we are involved in day in and day out without losing a second

For the mind not to get into thoughts, it has to be focused on some action. Given that we breathe continuously through our lifespan, breathing looks like a good base to focus on. We have to just keep observing our breathing. Thoughts will be there, but they will take a back seat when the mind is focused on observing the breathing. What happens over time is, you will start observing how your body behaves when you breathe. You will have an inner understanding of how your body is performing at both physical and mental level, and yet be at peace with it

Once the mind is focused on your breathing, you will start to observe things around you with clarity and in depth. Although slow and deep breathing helps the mind to focus more, a starter can just observe his/her way of breathing which makes the mind focus. You may hear sounds around you which you had never heard before, or observe other living beings from an angle which deepens your understanding of yourself and your surroundings.

The brain starts to learn new aspects of living and life. Learning is food for the brain. Stored information creates a barrier for the brain to learn. Mindfulness removes that barrier by observing things in their true form.

When the mind works in harmony with the self and the surrounding in pure action in the moment, that flow state gets created

Will this happen immediately when you start to be aware? The mind has got into the habit of thinking. We have to train the mind to be aware in this moment by focusing it on our breathing or any other object/work of our interest. Any action becomes a habit when it is continued on a daily basis for a long period of time

For starters, an easy way to bring the mind to focus is to head right into chaos and try to focus the mind on every action happening. We can go into a nearby park where people come for a walk/jog. We just have to sit there and make the mind focus on the actions happening around us. The footsteps, the breathing, people talking, birds chirping, wind flow etc. When the mind starts to focus and goes past the threshold of annoyance, the mind will by itself start to observe these actions deeply. The mind can tell us how fast a person is walking by observing the footsteps, where the bird is chirping from, which direction and how fast the wind is flowing. When this happens, we feel a fresh sense of awareness and aliveness. The feeling brings deeper relaxation than a good night's sleep. Such is the power of awareness

Productive Days

Awareness creates the flow required to focus on the work at hand restricting the mind to get into thoughts. Work doesn't mean physical work or knowledge work. Remember, work in our perspective points out to Living. Bringing in awareness in Living is a hard task given how the mind works

Productivity is being talked about all over the World. Why productivity in the first place? We are trying to look deep into this aspect here. Being productive means to add value to the work we do and complete it to satisfaction. In professional work where monetary compensation is involved, productivity points out towards utilizing time effectively to add value to the work we do

But, can we be productive by ourselves? By ourselves, we mean to be productive in Living. Can we be able to do that? If yes, how? How can we introduce productivity in Living?

Awareness of every moment of our day-to-day lives helps us to be productive. Productivity, in this context, is enjoying every moment of our Life! How can we enjoy every moment when we are surrounded by chaos which makes us stressed, you may ask. Awareness creates that flow which helps us observe and understand every moment of our interaction with the World, which brings in deeper learning and wisdom. We start to understand the deeper meaning of our interactions with ourselves and the outside environment. This continued awareness creates the energizing loop of deeper

understanding and learning which creates a positive flow. This deeper understanding creates the joy of Living

When we become productive at Living, other aspects like being productive at work look easier, because we have already created the flow of positivity. Of course, scheduling your days for our work needs to be done, but once we are in flow state, we can be sure of enjoying our days and making them productive

Smiling has a deep positive effect on the mind. We often see erratic behavior from ourselves when we get disturbed or troubled by others. We can clearly see the role of the mind here, but having a smile on our face through such situations can help us in flowing through such situations rather than reacting to them. You should try it for yourself. Try to smile through difficult situations or throughout the day. You will see that you flow through the situations and get work done effectively. The act of smiling tells the mind that you are enjoying the situation rather than getting stressed. It is like tricking the mind into believing everything is going good! Which is in fact, how it should be! Smiling through the day can be a very productive tool for ourselves!

Productive experts today talk about controlling the outside environment, but they seldom talk about managing the mind to create this flow state. This is why we see the plans for productivity failing

When we understand that change has to start from within us, we can truly transform ourselves

IN US LIES THE PROBLEM. IN US LIES THE SOLUTION

www.ingramcontent.com/pod-product-compliance
Lightning Source LLC
LaVergne TN
LVHW050409160726
843469LV00041B/1006

* 9 7 8 9 3 5 4 5 8 6 6 3 7 *